Office Politics 101

Silencing Of The Back Stabbing Lambs.

(BOOK 3 OF THE SERIES... " HAPPY JOB HUNTING")

ETHAN POWERS

Workforce Development Collection

Funded by
The California State Library
Initiatives Book Project

RIVERSIDE
PUBLIC LIBRARY

HAPPY JOB HUNTING SERIES BOOK
Other related books on your career are:

BOOK 1 - <u>Common Interview Questions</u>
To cut and paste:
http://www.amazon.com/dp/B00LBA3398
(Contains more than 100 model Q & A and the psychology behind the questions)

BOOK 2 - <u>The Unspoken Interview Question That ALL Interviewer Will Ask</u>
To cut and paste:
http://www.amazon.com/dp/B00NJU72XQ
(Learn how to answer the nonverbal question which is extremely critical in all interviews).

TABLE OF CONTENTS

Introduction

Discover how to describe a circle as being a square. This is politics.

Chapter 1: Office Politics 101

Why office politics exist and why you cannot avoid it.

Chapter 2: The General Purpose Antidote Pill

Three attributes that will neutralize any politics being played.

Chapter 3: Thirty Political Games & Tips

More than 30 situations you may encounter and how to manage them.

Conclusion

One Last Thing

Please, please, please.

Copyright Stuff

Introduction

When there is smoke, there is fire. Similarly, when there is work, there is office politics.
Office politics are present in every workplace. What differs is the degree of severity.

This book is for everyone that is in employment or about to get hired.
Allow me to attract the attention of the non-believers first.
For those readers that do not want to be involved or do not believe in office politics, think again.
Recall your school days... have you seen bullies picking on innocent boys and girls?
As humans, there is always someone who will bully the weaker ones to feed their ego.

OK, let's continue and this is for all of you.
A lot of talented and diligent professionals do not get the position they deserve just because they fail to properly play office politics. Partly, they can't be blamed. The term *office politics* has gained a negative connotation. Most professionals associate it with cheating, back lashing and taking advantage of other people. Therefore, a lot of them stay away from office politics. However, this conservative move can be detrimental to their careers. What they fail to

accept is that there will always be other factors that influence a person's career growth other than talents and skills. Office politics will prevail regardless if you chose to accept it or ignore it.

Fresh graduates may be the first victims of negative office politics. Most of them are unaware of the unspoken rules and culture in the workplace. Office politics are not formally taught in schools and universities, so most young professionals do not know how to handle negative office politics directed against them.

Have you ever been a topic of gossip? Are you being undercompensated for your work? Are you surrounded by difficult and toxic colleagues? Are you constantly given tasks that seem like a dead end while others receive easy projects? You could be playing office politics to your disadvantage. Whether you are a neophyte or a tenured professional, you should play office politics well with dignity. It is inevitable to get along with sly professionals in the course of your career, so it is just as important to have defensive strategies as well.

This book will give you tips and helpful insights on how to play office politics to gain a better life in your workplace. It contains enumerated tips on how to handle certain office situations. You can read these easy-to-follow tips anytime and anywhere.

I was fortunate to be introduced to office politics at my first job. The degree of backstabbing was very high in that company which in turn became a benchmark for the rest of my career. Fortunately, when I switch jobs, all my other jobs did not have such a high level of office politics.

It has been more than 25 years since my first job but I can clearly remember the words that my manager spoke about office politics.

He drew a circle on the whiteboard, pointed to it and said " Ethan, if you can describe this as a square, then you are there."

I have to admit that to this day, I can't achieve it. At most I am able to describe it as an ellipse.

In a sense, the colleagues that engaged in workplace politics are frightened little lambs. They feel inadequate and insecure. Office politics is a way to mask their true emotions but at the expense of others.

It is my sincere wish that after reading this book, you are able to silence these lambs in a good way so that you are not manipulated by them.

Here are the snippets of the various chapters.

Chapter 1... explains why office politics exist.
Chapter 2... covers the cure in general. It applies
to most situations and it would enable you to
have a good foundation in any career. It is like
taking a daily dose of your multi-vitamin pill.
Chapter 3... contains more than 30 wonderful
general tips for everybody who is working or
about to find a job.
After reading this chapter, you will find that
working life is more fun, enjoyable, less stress
and along the way, most likely you will get
promoted faster.

Chapter 1: Office Politics 101

The reason why office politics exist is because each employee has his own agenda or interest at work.
It may be due to the need for power, influence, recognition, reward or getting things done in their favor.
Or it can be just pure jealousy or bullies.
Another common cause is to cover up one's own error at the expense of you.

The most prevalent political game would be the need for power, as it would mean that you are in control. According to Tony Robbins, power or significance is one of the six basic human needs. Successful or high achievers are often people in power, for example world leaders like Adolf Hitler or Winston Churchill.
The higher you are in the corporate ladder, the higher the political game is played.

The second most popular reason is for career advancement.
A colleague will play office politics in order to climb the corporate ladder, otherwise it will take a long, long time for the promotion.

The third most popular reason is getting things done in their favor. For example, in trying to avoid doing additional tasks or eyeing for the job posting in a new district.

The next popular reason is just human nature... jealousy.
All it takes is for you to be prettier or better looking than someone and that person may feel jealous.
So you see, it may not even be work related!
Another possible trigger point is when you are compared with another worker. You may be doing your work quietly but the moment your boss mentioned something good about you to another co-worker, he may get jealous.
This is like when your parents compared you to your siblings.." Kid, why can't you be like your sister? She's so good at her studies while you slouch all day reading comic books."

The next one is related to your boss. If your boss is selfish or narrow-minded or if you have the potential to take over his position someday, he will play politics to gain the upper hand and keep you suppressed.

Last but not least, it is very common that there is always a shortage of manpower in any department. If additional or adhoc work crops up, the manager may have no choice but to employ political strategies to get other department to do the job.

Failure to push away the additional workload would mean that his subordinates will have to do the work and this will create unhappiness or frustration for his subordinates.

Chapter 2: The General Purpose Antidote Pill

Below are countermeasures that are universal which can be used in most of the cases to neutralize the office politics

Antidote #1: - Your personality or interpersonal skills.
Some of you may not believe it but your personality is the greatest weapon against office politics. Be humble, approachable and make as many friends as possible. Next are your communication skills. This refers to both your verbal and nonverbal.

Once I watched a video of the Dalai Lama's visit to a hotel. He greeted everyone, from the Manager to the Doorman with the same warmth energy. His smile, handshake and greetings are amazingly consistent. There is no sign that he is more superior or more knowledgeable than the Managers, the cooks or the chambermaids.
You can feel the staff reciprocated his greetings with much enthusiasm and positiveness. This is humbleness at its best.
Everyone is a fellow human being, no labeling.

The next one…" make friends, not enemies with everyone" can be told in the following story. Once upon a time, there was a large multinational company that employed a Principal Engineer, who holds a Ph. D. Mr. Scott is highly respected but he is quite power crazy. In meetings, you can observe that he wants to be in control and every time someone suggests a better solution, he will override with alternatives. Then one day, a big technical problem surfaced and is costing the company a huge loss daily as production of the component is severely affected with a low yield. Months pass by with no hope of any solution.

Then along came a Manager, who works in a sub-contractor company. The subcontractor is involved in the project and the Manager is tasked to work with Mr. Scott.

No matter how the Manager suggested various solutions, they are turned down.

Finally the Manager offered Mr Scott a solution but he told Mr. Scott that the solution was just an extension of one of the solutions that Mr. Scott had mentioned previously. In other words, the Manager painted the picture that the original idea came from Mr. Scott.

It worked, the solution was implemented and the problem was solved.

Mr. Scott got the credit, not the Manager but what the manager gained was far more valuable. They became great friends and even became golf buddies. All future work became a collaboration and other workers can see that the Manager has won the respect of Mr. Scott..

I know the story because the manager's name is Ethan Powers.

Antidote #2: - Your communication skills
Often misunderstanding and misinterpretation can be minimized just by your communication skills.

Suppose you communicated with a colleague and the understanding is that she will undertake a certain task. A week passes by and to your surprise, it was not done.

Whose fault is it?

Let's read another short story and see if you can pick up the message.

The great war guru, Sun Tzu was nominated by the king to lead the army. He was nominated to be the general only after he demonstrated one of his principle in the Art of War.

Before he demonstrated his skill, he made the King promise that the King will not interfere with his work.

He summoned all the king's concubines to the yard and commanded them to march in formation. He shouted, "Left, right, left, right!" None of the concubines moved and giggles can be heard all over.

Sun Tzu said. " When an instruction is given and the soldiers did not obey or understand, it is the commander's fault."

He then shouted out again...," Left, right, left, right."

The giggles grew louder.

"When the instruction is repeated and the soldiers continue to disobey, it is the soldiers' fault. Guards, behead the lead concubine for disobeying orders!" shouted Sun Tzu. The King was horrified, and there was dead silence for a moment. He wanted to stop the execution but remembered the promise. With a deep sigh, he just watched helplessly and in despair.

After the execution, Sun Tzu gave the command once again." Left, right, left, right."

This time the concubines marched without hesitation.

The King was saddened by the loss of the concubine but deep down, he knew that Sun Tzu would make a great general.

So, can you spot the lesson, which applies to this day and in any dialogue?

Here it is... when we communicate and the other party fails to understand the message, it is our fault.To repeat or to reconfirm is always an excellent way to ensure that your message is understood.
I make it a point to ask my Engineers to repeat what I say to them for critical tasks.

Incidentally, do read books on The Art of War by Sun Tzu. The principles are priceless and you can apply them at work or even at home.
Here is another great principle..." Know yourself, know your enemy, a thousand battles fought, a thousand battles won."
The meaning is that you must know your strengths and weaknesses and also the other party that you are interacting. The other party can be anyone, your boss, colleagues, your spouse or your children.
Often we tend to focus on the other party and are ignorant to look at ourselves in the equation.

The nonverbal communication skill is equally important. If you have read Book 2 of this series, you can appreciate the importance of body language and nlp

Antidote #3: Anti- Stress

Another valuable trait to master is the ability to handle stress.

Make an effort in this important area. The more you accelerate your car, the more the exhaust smoke is produced. It is a byproduct of travelling faster. Similarly, the higher you are in your career, the higher the stress level.

Learn anti-stress techniques like meditation or NLP.

It took me six weeks before I could meditate consistently every day. Now if I miss meditating three days straight in a row, I feel uneasy. It is as if I did not take a shower.

An awesome statement by Tony Robbins that you can consider is " nothing has any meaning, except the meaning that you give".

In any unfavorable situation, it is up to you to give it an empowering or disempowering meaning.

Summary of the All-Purpose Antidote

The three attributes that can help you neutralize almost any political game that is being played: (The acronym **CIA**...communication, interpersonal and anti-stress).

- Your communication skills
- Your interpersonal skills

- Your anti-stress level or ability to handle stress..

Shall we proceed to Chapter 3 now, where specific situations are laid out?

CHAPTER 3: The 30 Tips On Political Games

Tip #1: Know that Office Politics is Inevitable

Worth repeating this.
Office politics are an indispensable part of the working life. Unlike in schools and universities where people can ignore each other if they do not feel like getting along with them, employees must be able to interact with each other. It is a natural scenario in the office for employees to compete with each other. The majority of your colleagues wants to be promoted. However, everyone is working with limited resources. Because of this, things can get dirty. Some of your colleagues will not have doubts about tricking someone in order to gain advantage.

Tip #2: Know Your Surroundings

A secret of being powerful is to have a lot of connections. That way, when one tries to severe your ties, you still have other connections. As much as possible, you should try to have connections or friends on every hierarchy in your workplace. Your relationship with them should be built on respect and trust. Avoid empty and shallow flattery at all costs. Be mindful that your connections will be asking help from you, too, so be ready to lend a hand.

Tip #3: Sticky Business

Some people in the workplace will always be obsequious because they have nothing to offer. They basically have no talent or productive trait. As a result, they rely aggressively on office politics in order to leverage their faults and gain favors of superiors in order to be advanced, promoted or recognized. These people will not hesitate to use others to their advantage. They will suddenly be kind to you and spend time getting to know you, perhaps at lunch and coffee breaks. Then they will ask if you can do something for them. Once done, it's as if they have forgotten about you. Keep your friends close and your enemies closer.

Tip #4: Get to Know Your Enemies

You feel safe with your trusted friends in the workplace and most probably, threatened by your enemies; but if you distance yourself too much from your enemies, you will be left unaware of their motives. With your knowledge of these, you will be familiar of how they are likely to play with whatever is at their disposal in order to achieve their goals. In order to maneuver yourself safely in the politics of your workplace, you have to know not just your friends, but also your enemies. Take time to know them better but be extremely cautious of what you say.

Tip #5: What to Do when Faced with a Tunnel Vision

When you are caught in a situation of conflict about work-related planning, it is very easy to have a limited sight of things. This is called tunnel vision. You will limit your perception only to things that you want to see. When there is a conflict among people in the same or different departments, it can be difficult to be not personal about it. Let go of your personal interest and look at the bigger picture.

Tip #6: Prioritize The Company's Motives

The primary concern of your office is the motives of the company. When you are caught in an argument, take some time to remember and ponder on the objectives of the corporation. Sometimes, no matter how good a suggestion or a strategy sounds like, when it is against the business objectives, they may need reconsideration. In some cases, they should not be pushed at all. In any business-related decision, you should always keep in mind business objectives.

Tip #7: What Do You Think About It?

Some people in your workplace naturally know how to take the credit for somebody's work or effort. One of their styles is coming to you in a seemingly engaging or motivating conversation. They will bring up topics such as business proposals and feasibilities and act as if they are impressed with what you have to say. They will urge you to tell them more. Often, these conversation topics are about the nature of the work assigned to them. In some cases, they may even ask for research or reliable data to back up your claims. As a result, you will end up working for them without any credit. Do not be docile and know if you're being taken advantage of.

Tip #8: Realize Who You Work For

You can't just do someone a favor and let them take credit for it, regardless if they are your friends or not. If you encountered someone who wants to make you work on something your boss did not delegate to you, let your boss know. Tell your boss that your colleague came up with an idea for a project and that he asked you to do the research about, for example, the income bracket and preferences of the target audience. In the office, learn to distinguish the wolves and the wolves dressed up as sheep so you can avoid being one of the victims of politics.

Tip #9: Fake Back-Up Support

Most people will use the assurance of support and encourage you to take risks. When you are about to undertake a risk, they will assure you that they are right behind you in case troubles arise. Sometimes, they will even encourage you to take uncalculated risks and tell you the possible benefits and advantages if you took that risk. Ask yourself: if it is so good, why aren't they taking the risk themselves? These people can go as far as making promises about a great advance in your career if you took that risk.

Tip#10: Always Research First

Read more about a risk involved in a project before deciding to be part of it. If you are dealing with other companies, take the time to read their track records and customer feedback. Know the available time you have between your actual work load and your personal life. You don't want to be stuck on something just because you realized you can't manage to balance your priorities. It's not worth taking if you have to sacrifice too much of your health, money and effort. Do not allow your emotions to decide for you. Take a look at the benefits and the effort you have to do in exchange for it. Lastly, trust your gut feeling. No matter how good a project sounds like, there can be something inside you that urges you not to be part of it.

Tip #11: Deliberate Doom

As mentioned before, some people in your workplace will use any kind of trick in order for them to advance better than you. One of their tricks includes deliberately withdrawing vital information from their colleagues so that they will be misled into taking action. The sly employee may take away important clauses, terms and prerequisites in presentations and reports. Do not believe easily in anything. Be critical but don't exactly voice out your doubts. Be mysterious.

Tip#12: Know the Classic Office Gossip Style: Photocopier Message

Call it immature, but some people will purposely leave documents around the photocopier machine for someone to discover and hopefully spread rumors about. The management may not necessarily and genuinely issue these documents. Sometimes, these people will print fabricated gossips and even controversial pictures. This is one of the reasons why having a lot of genuine connections is important. Once you have people on all hierarchy in the corporation who care about your professional well-being, it will be hard for someone to pull you down. A person who is known for his dignity is hard to shatter with gossips. Extend this sense of dignity in your personal life as well. Do not get into office affairs. Cultivate a healthy image so these photocopy machine tactics will not work with you.

Tip #13: Keep Calm When Faced With Hateful Criticisms

In the office world, it is natural that a person or a group of people will hate you if you have achieved something. They will hate you so much to the point of committing offenses against you that are below the belt. The most human reaction is to retaliate in the same measure, which involves committing below the belt offenses, too. Your boss or your supervisor is expecting this to happen, and one stupid move in order to defend your honor is enough to cause you to be dismissed, suspended or fired. In the end, you can't defend yourself against the management if you committed such offense. Develop a good reputation and practice self-control. Show them you're unaffected.

Tip#14: Be Unpredictable And Smart.

Go beyond the expectation of anyone who you did offend. They will hate you and bash you in the hope that you will feel down and discouraged. Worse, they are waiting for you to retaliate. In case you did retaliate with below the belt offenses, they will find the opportunity to reveal your offensive act to your boss. One rational approach is to talk to the person who offended you (assuming you know who really offended you). Don't do anything that is expected of you by the time they offended you. Feel neutral about the offensive blows and pretend to be discouraged. Let the offended get tired with his bashing then strike him with your success. This will make the people doubt the credibility of the offender's claims and the next time people bash you, they will be less believable.

Tip#15: Intentional Exclusions

Generally, an office or a department has a list of people to whom the person in charge will send important messages and announcements for meetings. Some people will delete or erase a person's name off the list so that he or she will miss important meetings and special announcements. It is a big deal for the boss if his employees miss meetings. One missed meeting without due notice is detrimental to an employee's professional image. On the first chance of a missed meeting, approach the person in charge and tell your boss about the incidence.

Tip #16: In Case Of No Notifications

The very first incidence that you missed a special announcement or a notice for a general assembly, approach the secretary and ask why you missed it. Most corporations send emails, but some companies are gradually using SMS to disseminate information. If you still miss announcements after this, then approach your boss and tell him your concern. It could be that a colleague who hates you asked the secretary to omit your name from the list.

Tip # 17: The Boss Strikes

Sometimes, it is your own boss who ruins your every day. Other times, it could be your company's clients. It can be hard to turn down tasks from your boss, even if these tasks are totally irrelevant to your position. For example, how do you turn down your boss's request to arrange her 4-year-old's birthday party? Learn to respect yourself. Gently turn down your boss's irrational requests especially if you haven't built a rapport with him yet. Be polite to prevent hostility.

Tip #18: Stand your Guard

If the management is starting to be too stressful for you to handle, turn your focus to your circle of influence. These are the group of people who are willing to help you by showing you ways on how to complete a task. You should be fond of politely saying "no" when you have to, otherwise people will see you as someone who makes excuses to avoid tasks. To balance things out, learn to accept only requests that you believe will contribute to your professional skills and expansion of connections.

Tip#19: Know what to do when you Receive Rotten Tomatoes

There will be an office incident wherein someone will delegate the tasks and projects that are an inevitable failure to the employees or managers he dislikes. He will then assign easy or highly productive tasks to his favorites so they will advance faster. This can be hard to avoid because you cannot control a person's decision. This may be difficult to counter once someone is already assigned a doomed task. Therefore, the wisest approach to this is to do the task nevertheless. If the task really seems like a dead end, do feasibility studies and ask around if the particular task has already been taken but was declined in the past. Don't be afraid to add some suggestions to make the task easier.

Tip #21: Stop Whining

Whining about a task or situation will only make them appear 10x more awful. If it's you who always gets the "cursed" tasks, then it's time to improve your connections. You may be getting leftover projects because the good ones were already delegated to people who are close to the management. Stop whining and improve those tasks. You may even get your boss's attention, which may warrant you for promotion.

Tip#22: What Are Psychological Demons?

There are subtle players in the workplace who try to weaken their rivals by playing tricks with their minds. Besides, a person can only do as much as he thinks he can. That certain employee will do his best to distract you so you cannot perform well. He will also try to discourage you so you will not assert yourself too much. These people are very toxic to be with. Nevertheless, you should know how to read them to predict them and turn their efforts against themselves. If they succeed, you will feel shy and unworthy of your accomplishments. Gradually, they will turn you into a people pleaser. Know your worth and do not be affected by blunt intimidation.

Tip #23: Always Guard Your Mind

A wise professional always guard his mind against the world. Not everything you hear or see is true. Take any criticism that they hurl at you and analyze them objectively. Sometimes, they could be telling the truth. The people who use psychological tactics will rarely harm their colleagues through gossips. Rather, they will go straight to the person, act with authority and try to shatter that person's confidence and drive to succeed. Be highly aware of these people because they are very clever in instilling negative thoughts about yourself. What's worse is that they often populate managerial positions so it is impossible not to interact and receive commands from them.

Tip #24: Stress Statement Number One — "You are too"

This statement is part of the psychological demons but needs to be expounded more. As mentioned before, constructive criticism is not detrimental to your skills. However, most people do not know what exactly a constructive criticism is. They take a mere criticism or prejudice as constructive criticism. In the workplace, you will often encounter the statement "you are too..." These statements are used in constructive criticism, too; but abusive people will use "you are too" in order to transform your strengths or assets into weaknesses and insecurities. For example, he says that you are too detail oriented. It means that he can't cope with your strength so he transforms it to a liability. He knows that you can advance yourself with this trait, so he will try to downplay it.

Tip #25: Stress Statement Number Two — "You need to be more"

Some people will tell someone to be more, for example, strategic. People who tell others to be more of something are usually basing their preferences on themselves. So for example, people who tell you to be more strategic want you to become strategic because they are strategic. If you will look at this approach from one angle, it may appear helpful. However, do not be misled. Some people want you to become like them so they can control you. Being strategic is a skill they have already mastered. If you try to become one, you will work under his influence, making you work for him in the end.

Tip #26: Know When To Be Critical

Always practice critical thinking. Do not easily accept what others are telling you to become. Likewise, look at the "faults" they point out at you. Are they really faults? If so, how? What is your end goal? What kind of employee do you want to become? If you were to become a boss, how would you want your employees to be? Likewise, if you have received the "you need to be more" speech, analyze the traits that you were told to be more of. If you were told to be more relaxed with your work and you realize that you barely give time to your family, they are probably right.

Tip #27: Doing What Professionals Do — Assert Yourself

Your workplace is not a venue for shy people. Even if they are diligent or smart, shy people will easily be overpowered. Learn to assert yourself. Mention your achievements, preferences and strengths if they are relevant. Decline something if you need to. There is one word of caution when you start to assert yourself. All those people who can't control you will start to get irritated by you. They will hate you because they can't get you to act the way they want. Some will stop bothering you, others will continue to pester you with other dirty tactics.

Tip #28: Promises Under Your Name

"But I promised them that you will do it"— does this sound familiar to you? Such people know that you have a weakness or a soft spot for not fulfilling promises. This will prompt them to use this weakness in order to get a job done by you. As a consequence, you are trapped by an other person's promise under your name. If you failed, it's your fault. If you succeeded, they will probably take the credit. If you didn't agree on doing a task, don't do it. If you didn't deliver, it's not your fault. It's the person who made the promise whose reputation will be tinged. Inform your boss or the management if someone promises that you allegedly claimed a task.

Tip #29: The Professional World Is Harsh On People Pleasers

Stop being a people pleaser. The fact that you are coaxed into committing yourself to a task for the sake of pleasing other people shows that you have a weak reputation in the office. You are most likely playing by other people's rules. Start asserting yourself by strengthening your political power. You can do this by reinforcing your relationships with other people in your workplace, regardless of position. People who are victims of psychological demons (see Tip #22) tend to be people pleasers. In the workplace, you have your own identity. You are more mature now so quit living to the expectations of people who don't care about your life and your career.

Tip#30: Forced Late Night Shift

Sometimes, it is inevitable to work for extended periods because your boss needs to rush results. This is particularly common as Holiday nears where most offices are closed. However, when you receive the "you have to work late tonight" line more often than usual, then you have to be alert. This is a selfish tactic. Yes, overtime hours must be paid and employees can opt to work overtime if they want to. However, you have a personal life, like any other human out there. If the person who wants you to work late will also work late with you, chances are he does not want to be lonely. He feels like you are the exact target who will easily agree on working late.

Tip #31: Meet Silent Susie

Silent Susie is hard to deal with. First, she will entertain your inquiries, proposals and suggestions as well. Then suddenly she stops responding to your calls and emails. You may see her around the office and tell her about your calls and emails. She will tell you that she's busy and that she will reply as soon as she can, but she never will. You noticed that Silent Susie stopped replying after you have sent her a few emails or phone calls. This is because you have exposed a part of your proposal that will not work to Susie's advantage.

Your suggestion may even emphasize her weaknesses. Susie wants something that will make her look good. Turn your proposals instead to your circle of influence, that way, they can provide more insights to it. Compare your proposals to the objectives of the company. However, be careful about the "tell me more about it" person (see Tip#7). Assuming that your influential group means well for your success, they can help propel this project from happening.

Tip #32: How To Handle Temper Tantrums

In the office, it could be hard not to take things personally, especially if someone suddenly sabotages your work and your reputation. Having an outburst of anger in order to retaliate may be satisfying —at first. Whatever happens, do not take office politics personally. Office politics exist because of power play. Most people in the office probably do not even care about their colleague's personal life. Therefore, learn to hold back your anger. Do not lash out on someone just because they took credit for your work or they sabotaged your project. In the future, you might need something from the person who sabotaged you. Knowing how to control your anger is good for your career.

Tip #33: Do You Have to Take Sides?

There might be a time when two of your colleagues will come up to you so you can be a middleman to them. They will try to argue with each other and hope that you will bring them on a common ground. You like the other person more, but if you take one side, you will be at risk of appearing biased. This will open the chance for them to blame you for any failure that may come up in the future because you made a decision that the other person is correct. Do not take any of their sides. They know deeply that their plans or preferences may be faulty. In short, they are not sure about it so they come up to you to mediate them. Put the company's objectives as a basis.

Tip #34: How Your Boss's Perception Of You Affects Your Career

There is barely an objective measure of how your boss judges you as an employee. Your achievements, performance and promptness may beautify your image to your boss but what if he doesn't like you? Many talented people are stuck in their job with little recognition because they missed on playing with the workplace politics. Promotion and pay also depends on how the superiors perceive you. According to Oliver James' book, *Office Politics*, there is a triumvirate of traits that most people have in the workplace. These traits are narcissism (vain selfishness), Machiavellianism (manipulative and sly game-playing) and psychopathy (ruthlessness). A person who doesn't know how to maneuver his way around these 3 traits will most likely miss promotion, raise and career advancement. Always be aware of these negative traits.

Tip #35: Gossipy You

Perhaps you have been caught in the middle of a gossip session and you didn't want to participate by saying more detrimental lies (or facts) about someone. If you try to keep quiet, then your colleagues might try to grill you because they think you know something more. If you tried to correct their gossipy attitude and appear holy, they would resent you. One way of staying out of gossip when you are caught in a gossipy group is to divert the topic to something related to the gossip. Subtly change the topic, but don't go too far. The most important thing is that you should always stay out of gossips.

Tip#36: The Importance of Written Records

Nothing makes things easier than having a written record of matters. Written records, whether they be in a form of email or a paper document, has the power to save jobs and prevent further problems from developing. You should document your own accomplishments and highlight your strengths in each accomplishment. Write your responsibilities in a task. If you work in a group, document the progress of your project. Record down who did a certain task. Always back up official documents. If need be, keep a print screen of a picture file.

Tip# 37: Monkey See, Monkey Do

People will always follow the acts of someone subconsciously. It is a common saying that you are the sum of the 5 people you hang out the most. While this is not entirely true, there is still truth to this. Hang out with gossipy people and pretty soon you will be a gossiper yourself. Hang out with cheaters and you will slowly begin to cheat little by little, not just in your work. Surround yourself with people who you want to be. They should motivate you, inspire you and give you a healthy challenge from time to time.

It doesn't necessarily mean that you should be friends with them at first, but gradually they would be. Just as surrounding yourself with influential people, having a boss with an honest, hard-working and resilient character will motivate you and other employees to be like him. How do you feel if you have a lousy, incompetent and pessimistic boss? If you are the boss, set a good example to your staff.

Tip #38: How to Toot your Own Horn

Have you ever wondered why nobody has noticed your efforts and skills so far? This may be due to your lack of projecting yourself forward. Be confident to highlight your skills and contribution to the management. Don't do it in a bragging or desperate tone, as if you deserve to be rewarded. Rather, emphasize how your efforts have contributed to the company's objectives. The management has so many things to take care of therefore, an employee's achievement may go unnoticed. Tooting your own horn may not please some people, but it is better to try to be noticed.

Tip #39: Trick Question. What Do You Dislike About the Company?

There are some people in the office who will engage in a casual and even friendly conversation with you. They will direct the topic to the company's shortcoming and wait for you to complain. They will nod in agreement, only to pass your complaints to your boss or to the management. It is important to practice tact all the time. Keep some of your thoughts to yourself. Do not rant and carelessly backstab the management and your colleagues just because someone asked for your opinion.

Conclusion

Office politics can either make or break you. Every working man and woman should know how to play office politics well to their advantage in order to get along with their colleagues and managers. In the workplace, it is inevitable for a conflict to arise between two people. Many people risk derailing their careers off track just because they do not know how to handle workplace conflict well. Knowing even just the basics of good office politics teaches you how to avoid and resolve petty fights.

Being knowledgeable and active in office politics does not mean pushing others down in order to gain a premier spot. Rather, it is about widening your networks by building relationships inside and outside the company. It will help you choose the people to invest your time with. Participating in office politics is also about informing others about your contributions to the company and welcoming help and criticism. This may sound self-serving at first, but in order to advance your career, you need to play office politics well. This will also help you gain control over your career.

At some point in your professional life, generally about 5 to 7 years, you will take on tasks that depend greatly on people around you. Therefore, it is crucial to secure proper connections and relationships as early as possible.

Office politics teach you the social psychology of being powerful. Once you get it right, it will make your career more than twice as fruitful.

One Last Thing

If you have benefitted from this book, you can add good karma for yourself and others by reaching out to other like-minded readers.

The way the system works, if you write a review about this book, it is like a beacon out at sea. The constant light will be seen by those searching for this book.
It does not take much time or effort to do a review, even a one-liner is sufficient.
Well, even a one word review is powerful enough.

Thank you and may you be well and happy.

ETHAN POWERS

http://www.EscalateYourCareer.com/

Text Copyright © Ethan Powers

All rights reserved. No part of this guide may be reproduced in any form without permission in writing from the publisher except in the case of brief quotations embodied in critical articles or reviews.

Legal & Disclaimer

The information in this book has been provided for educational and entertainment purposes only.

The information contained in this book has been compiled from sources deemed reliable and it is accurate to the best of the Author's knowledge; however, the Author cannot guarantee its accuracy and validity and cannot be held liable for any errors or omissions. Changes are periodically made to this book.

Upon using the information contained in this book, you agree to hold harmless the Author from and against any damages, costs and expenses, including any legal fees, potentially resulting from the application of any of the information provided in this guide. This disclaimer applies to any damages or injury caused by the use and application, whether directly or indirectly, of any advice or information presented, whether for breach of contract, tort, negligence, personal injury, criminal intent or under any other cause of action.

You agree to accept all risks of using the information presented in this book.